D0338497

DESERT

APRIL PULLEY SAYRE

Twenty-First Century Books

Brookfield, Connecticut

For my father, David Clarence Pulley, who always believed.
~ A.P.S. ~

ACKNOWLEDGMENTS

A special thanks to the scientists who reviewed all or part of the manuscript: Dr. James A. MacMahon of Utah State University, Dr. Dennie Miller of the Chihuahuan Desert Research Institute, and Dr. Paul Krausman of the University of Arizona.

Twenty-First Century Books
A Division of The Millbrook Press
2 Old New Milford Road
Brookfield, CT 06804

Text Copyright © 1994 by April Pulley Sayre
Illustrations Copyright © 1994 by Martha Weston
All rights reserved.

Library of Congress Cataloging-in-Publication Data
Sayre, April Pulley.
Desert / April Pulley Sayre.
p. cm. — (Exploring earth's biomes)
Includes index.
1. Desert ecology—Juvenile literature. 2. Deserts—Juvenile literature.
3. Desert ecology—North America—Juvenile literature. 4. Deserts—
North America—Juvenile literature. [1.Deserts. 2. Desert ecology. 3.
Ecology.] I. Title. II. Series: Sayre, April Pulley. Exploring earth's biomes.
QH541.5.DS49 1994   574.5'2652—dc20
                                                        94–21427

ISBN 0-8050-2825-0

Printed in the United States of America

10 9 8 7 6

Photo Credits
pp. 8, 16, 23 (left), 30, 31: Tom Bean; p. 15: U.S. Department of Interior, Death Valley National Monument; p. 22 (photo and inset): Jim Steinberg/Photo Researchers, Inc.; p. 23 (right): Sylvain Grandadam/Photo Researchers, Inc.; pp. 35, 40: Tom McHugh/Photo Researchers, Inc.; p. 49: Dan Budnik/Woodfin Camp & Associates, Inc.; p. 53: Lawrence Migdale/Photo Researchers, Inc.; p. 55: April Pulley Sayre.

CONTENTS

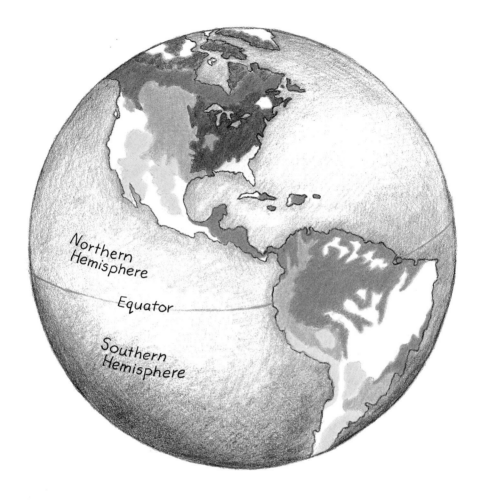

Northern
Hemisphere

Equator

Southern
Hemisphere

rain forest
grassland
desert
temperate deciduous forest
taiga
tundra

INTRODUCTION

Take a look at the earth as a whole and you'll see its surface can be divided into living communities called biomes. Desert, rain forest, tundra, taiga, temperate deciduous forest, grassland, and polar desert are some of the main terrestrial biomes—biomes on land. Each biome has particular kinds of plants and animals living in it. Scientists also identify other biomes not mentioned here, including aquatic biomes—biomes of lakes, streams, and the sea.

When their boundaries are drawn on a globe, terrestrial biomes look like horizontal bands stacked up from Pole to Pole. Starting from the equator and moving outward toward the Poles, you'll find rain forests, grasslands, deserts, and grasslands once again. Then things change a little. The next biomes we think of—temperate deciduous forests, taiga, and tundra—exist only in the Northern Hemisphere. Why is this true? Well, if you look in the Southern Hemisphere, you'll see there's very little land in the regions where these biomes would supposedly lie. There's simply nowhere for these biomes to exist! Conditions on small pieces of land—islands and peninsulas—that lie in these areas are greatly affected by sea conditions and are very different from those on continents.

But why do biomes generally develop in these bands? The answer lies in the earth's climate and geology. Climate is affected by the angle at which sunlight hits the earth. At the equator, sunlight passes through the atmosphere and hits the earth straight on, giving it its full energy. At the Poles, sunlight must pass through more atmosphere and it hits the earth at an angle, with less energy per square foot. Other factors also influence where biomes lie: the bands of rising and falling air that circulate around the planet; the complex weather systems created by jutting mountains, deep valleys, and cold currents; the glaciers that have scoured the lands in years past; and the activities of humans. This makes biome boundaries less regular than the simplified bands described above.

🌿 1 🌿
THE DESERT BIOME

In the United States it's Death Valley. In Saudi Arabia it's *Rub` al Khali*—the empty quarter. In China it's called *Takla Makan*—the place from which there is no return.

These desert areas are well named. Dry and often desolate, the desert can be a tough environment for humans. Sand dunes, bare rock, or pebbled ground can stretch for hundreds of miles, without a shady tree in sight. Travelers with enough water to survive the daytime heat may freeze on cool nights or become lost in dust and sandstorms.

Yet deserts aren't all dryness, dunes, and desolation. Deserts can have carpets of flowers, colorful birds, sudden floods, strange rock shapes, tree-sized cacti, salty lakes, and high mountains. And that's just a short list of their interesting features. The desert is a biome—a geographic area that has a certain kind of climate and a certain kind of community of plants and animals. But exactly what you'll see in a desert depends on which one you visit.

In the Sonora Desert of the southwestern United States, you'll find cacti in many sizes and shapes, from tiny pincushion cacti, to knee-high barrel cacti, to organ-pipe cacti that tower overhead. In the Australian Desert, you'll find an abundance of lizards, from 2-inch (5-centimeter) geckos to monitor lizards that can grow to be 7 feet (2 meters) long! In the Sahara Desert of northern Africa, you'll find 3.5 million hot, windy square miles (9 million square

The temperature drops quickly as the sun sets in the desert.

kilometers) of rock, pebbles, and sand with little wildlife. Yet its vast expanse has a special kind of beauty.

Despite their differences, deserts do have some things in common. By definition they're dry. On average, they receive less than 10 inches (25 centimeters) of precipitation a year. They also have a high evaporation rate, due to low humidity, solar radiation, and wind.

Deserts are lands of extremes—extreme dryness, sudden floods, hot days, and cold nights. To cope with these extreme conditions, desert organisms have some unusual features. There are animals that drink no water, plants that have no real leaves, and birds that soak their feathers to carry water many miles to their thirsty chicks.

For humans, deserts are also places of mystery. There are rocks that explode like gunshot and dunes that sing as the sand flows over them. There are sandstorms that build up so much static electricity that people within them feel ill. Above all, there are questions—questions and more questions—about the desert biome. Many remain unanswered.

8

TYPES

There are two main types of deserts: hot and cold.
- Hot deserts receive their precipitation as rain;
- Cold deserts receive their precipitation as snow.

Deserts are also classified by their aridity—their dryness. From wettest to driest, the classifications are: semi-arid, arid, hyper-arid.

TEMPERATURES

- Air temperature falls quickly at night and rises quickly during the day.
- Average yearly temperature range: 75°F (24°C) to 86°F (30°C).
- Below-freezing temperatures are not uncommon in deserts. Even hot deserts, such as the Sonora Desert in southwestern Arizona, occasionally get snow.

WEATHER

- Average humidity is low: 10 to 20 percent.
- Deserts average less than 10 inches (25 centimeters) of rain a year.
- Deserts have a high evaporation rate.
- Storms that do arrive may be strong; flash floods are not uncommon.
- Some deserts experience dust storms and windstorms.

SOIL

- Desert soils vary; they may be sandy, salty, crumbly, or very rocky.
- Many deserts have only pebbles at the surface, or just bare rock, and little real soil.
- Soil may be rich in minerals, but often lacks organic matter—decayed plants and animals.

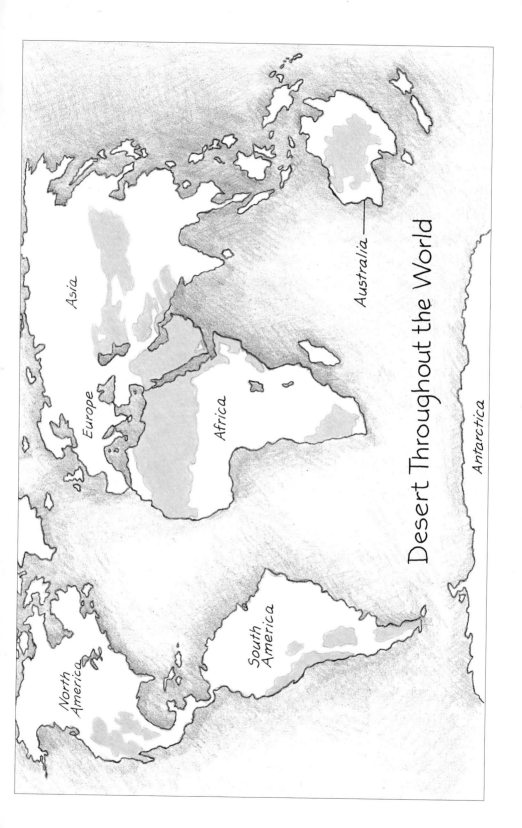

Desert Throughout the World

Asia

Europe

Africa

Australia

North America

South America

Antarctica

PLANTS

- Aboveground the desert's plant biomass—the total weight of plant matter—for a given area is generally lower than in other biomes.
- Often more biomass lies belowground—in roots—than above—in shoots, leaves, stems.
- Common plants: cacti, yucca, mesquite, sagebrush, saltbush, creosote bush, and a variety of annuals—non-woody plants that sprout, grow, produce seeds, and die all in one season.
- Plants have adapted to reduce water loss and increase water storage.

ANIMALS

- Some deserts have abundant wildlife, with large numbers of lizards and small mammal species.
- Animals have adapted to handle water scarcity and daytime heat.
- Animals exhibit convergent evolution—distantly related animals in different deserts of the world have separately evolved similar physical characteristics or behaviors.
- Drier deserts have fewer species; wetter ones have more.
- Hot deserts generally have more animal species than cold ones.

⚜ 2 ⚜
DESERT IN
NORTH AMERICA

On seeing the North American desert, a scientist from Egypt said, "To me this is not a desert, but a veritable botanical garden!" Indeed, in comparison to Egypt's Sahara, parts of the North American desert do seem lush.

Stretching from Idaho to as far south as the lowlands near Mexico City, the North American desert is diverse in its geology and biology. Scientists who classify deserts by their aridity consider this vast area to be semi-arid, on average. Yet specific spots, such as Death Valley, California, are hyper-arid, the driest classification. In some years, Death Valley gets no rain at all.

North American desert lands can be hot or cold, high or low, flat or mountainous. Only 2 percent of their area is sandy. The rest is a colorful variety of mountains, valleys, lakes, plateaus, and unusual rock forms. Much of the North American desert lies between the Sierra Nevada Range and the Rocky Mountains, in what geologists call the "Basin and Range Province." This area has many small mountain ranges with gently curving basins in between. Streams and rivers from these mountains flow into desert basins, creating lakes that often dry up in the desert heat.

Covering 493,000 square miles (1,277,000 square kilometers), the North American desert is generally considered to have four subdivisions: the Great Basin, the Mojave Desert, the Sonora Desert, and the Chihuahuan Desert. Each has its own characteristic features.

The Great Basin is called a cold desert because it receives over 60 percent of its precipitation as snow. The other three subdivisions of the North American desert are hot deserts, receiving most of their precipitation as rain. The distinctions among the three hot deserts are based primarily on the kinds of plants that live there. Still, their characteristic plant species overlap in some places.

For the most part, the wildlife of the three hot deserts is similar in form. Different species or subspecies may live in each desert, but they fill similar roles in the ecosystem. An ecosystem is made up of a living community of animals and plants and the physical environment—the rocks, air, water, and so on—around them. Within an average square mile, each of the hot deserts has 10 to 12 mammal species, 10 to 15 bird species, 10 to 20 reptile and amphibian species, and 300 to 500 arthropod species. (Arthropod species include not just insects, but also creatures such as spiders and scorpions.) North America's cold desert—the Great Basin—has fewer animal species than each of the three hot deserts.

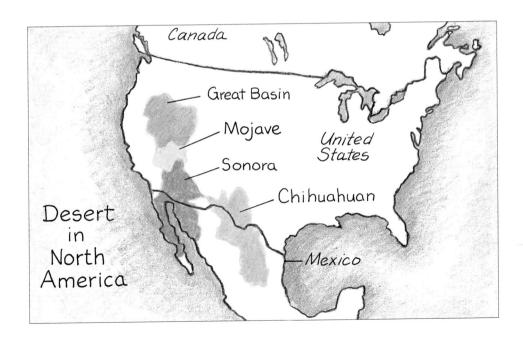

Canada

Great Basin

Mojave

United States

Sonora

Chihuahuan

Desert in North America

Mexico

GREAT BASIN

Area: 158,000 square miles (409,200 square kilometers)
Location: Nevada, Utah, Idaho, Oregon, and California
Main Precipitation: snow in winter
Plants: low shrubs, widely spaced, some adapted to salty soils; greasewood, sagebrush, shadscale, horsebrush, grasses
Desert Facts:

- Parts of the Great Basin were once covered with gigantic lakes. Most have dried up. The Great Salt Lake, which is 8 times saltier than the ocean, is the remainder of a lake that was 20 times its size.

- On the southeast edge of the Great Basin is an area called the Painted Desert, because of its colorful red and yellow rock formations. Here you'll find many of what we call our "desert" national parks—Canyonlands, Arches, Bryce Canyon, Grand Canyon, and others. But some scientists do not consider the Painted Desert a true desert. Although it has some desert plants, it also has patches of woodland and grassland vegetation.

MOJAVE DESERT

Area: 54,000 square miles (140,000 square kilometers)
Location: California, Nevada, Arizona, Utah
Main Precipitation: mostly rain in winter
Plants: low, widely spaced shrubs, such as creosote bush and white bursage, bright blooming winter annuals, a few low-growing cacti species, and yucca
Desert Facts:

- The Mojave's Death Valley is the hottest place in the United States, with an air temperature that once reached a record 134°F (56.7°C)! It's also the lowest place in the United States, at 282 feet (85.6 meters) below sea level. (Most of the Mojave is at a higher elevation and has more moderate temperatures.)

- The Joshua tree, a type of yucca that grows around the

The Joshua tree, native to the Mojave, is the largest yucca.

Mojave's edges, is often considered this desert's symbol. The Joshua Tree National Monument in California bears this plant's name.

SONORA DESERT

Area: 106,000 square miles (275,000 square kilometers)
Location: Arizona, California, and Mexico, including the Baja California peninsula
Main Precipitation: rain in winter and summer
Plants: diverse and plentiful—tall, columnar cacti such as saguaro and organ-pipe, shrubs such as creosote bush, taller shrubs such as mesquite, and a variety of winter and summer annuals
Desert Facts:
• The Sonora Desert is named for the Mexican state of Sonora, where the bulk of this desert lies.

- The Sonora's plant life is more abundant and its cacti more varied than almost any other desert in the world.

CHIHUAHUAN DESERT

Area: 175,000 square miles (450,000 square kilometers)
Location: Mexico, Arizona, New Mexico, and Texas
Main Precipitation: rainfall in winter
Plants: closely spaced shrubs such as creosote bush, many small cacti species, tall yucca and agave, lechuguilla, acacia trees, and summer annuals and grasses
Desert Facts:
- The Chihuahuan Desert is named for the Mexican state of Chihuahua, where part of this desert is located.
- The Chihuahuan Desert is cooler, with more rainfall than other hot deserts in the United States. Most of it is at higher elevations, too.

The organ-pipe cactus, common in Mexico, lives as far north as the Organ Pipe National Monument in southern Arizona.

3
DESERT WEATHER, CLIMATE, AND GEOLOGY

If you think deserts are quiet places where nothing ever happens, think again. In a desert you'll find raging rivers, swirling dust storms, rippling sands, and "ghostly" rain. And with few trees and plants around, there's not much covering the ground or blocking your view of the sky. So a desert is the perfect place to see wind, water, and weather at work, dramatically shaping the land.

DESERT WEATHER: HOT *AND* COLD

The desert is the hottest biome on earth. So if you're camping in a desert, bring cool, lightweight clothes and a sun hat. But bring a warm sweater, too. You may swelter in daytime temperatures over 100°F (38°C). But at night that sweater may come in handy when the temperature dips to 40–60°F (5–15°C).

The reason deserts heat up and cool off so quickly is because they're "bare" to the elements. They have no insulation. There's nothing to prevent them from heating up quickly in the sun, or cooling off quickly at night.

The Humidity Blanket   Most other biomes are insulated by their humidity—the water vapor in the air. A forested area may have 80 to 90 percent humidity in its daytime air. This water reflects and absorbs the sun's energy. It prevents much of this heat energy from reaching the ground. At night, the same water vapor acts like a blanket. It keeps some of the day's heat from escaping into the atmosphere.

Deserts, in contrast, have only 10 to 20 percent humidity. As a result, more of the sun's energy reaches the ground. The soil bakes. It gets so hot you really *could* fry an egg on the sidewalks in some desert towns! The ground surface can get to 165°F (74°C) during the summer. The pavement may get even hotter.

DESERTS: WET *AND* DRY

There's an old saying, "when it rains, it pours." This is doubly true for deserts. Deserts may get little rain on average. But they often get huge amounts all at once. Places in the Sahara may get rain only once in 20 years. But they can get a decade's worth in just a few hours. Conditions vary among deserts. While the Mojave experiences reliable, gentle winter rains, the Atacama Desert in Chile may go for years without a drop of rain.

Flash Flood! It may be sunny where you are, and that streambed nearby may look bone dry. But if it's raining upstream, beware! Flash floods can rip through the desert, turning dry streambeds and ditches into fast-moving streams within minutes. Almost every year, people in the desert are killed by floods when trying to walk or drive across streambeds.

Wacky Weather Deserts have some unusual weather events: ghost rain, dust storms, and sandstorms. A ghost rain happens when rain falls from a cloud but never reaches the soil. Water droplets hit a super-hot layer of air near the ground. *Psst!* The droplets evaporate.

Dust storms are stirred up by the wind. These dust clouds, thousands of feet high, can block out the sun.

Sometimes big storms carry red Saharan soils all the way from Africa to the rooftops of Paris. Stronger winds can pick up and carry larger particles, causing a sandstorm. Sand only gets about 6 ½ feet (about 2 meters) off the ground. But it can act like a sandblaster, grinding rocks smooth and stripping the paint from cars.

Both dust storms and sandstorms can, on occasion, kill people and other animals. The particles make it difficult to breathe. They can also quickly dehydrate an animal. Within a sandstorm, the friction of the sand particles rubbing against one another creates static electricity in the air. This electrically charged air can give people headaches.

HOW DESERTS FORM

If you look at the earth, you'll see that deserts aren't just randomly scattered around the globe. They are located where they are because of four main factors: subtropical belts, rain shadows, dry interiors, and cold currents.

Subtropical Belts   Most deserts lie in two belts. One belt is close to 30 degrees latitude north, and another is around 30 degrees latitude south. These areas, called the subtropics, have the perfect desert-forming climate. Because of the earth's shape, tilt, and surface features, the sun heats the earth unevenly. This uneven heating creates wind and causes large air masses to move around the earth. In the desert belts, large masses of dry air descend and warm. Once they're warmed, these air masses can hold more water, so they act like giant sponges. They absorb water from the land. Then, heated by the desert sun, they rise and move on.

Two other parts of the earth—the Arctic and Antarctic—have similar air masses. As a result, they are quite dry. They are sometimes called polar deserts. They are so cold that what precipitation they *do* get rarely evaporates.

Rain Shadows   Rain shadow deserts form when a mountain cuts off a low-lying area's rain supply, leaving it in a "shadow" where it gets little rain. Here's how a rain shadow works: As moist air sweeps up and over mountains, it cools. Once it has cooled, the air cannot hold as much water vapor as it could when it was warm. So the water in the air condenses, forms clouds, and rains down. The rain falls on the ocean side and top of the mountain. By the time the air reaches the other side of the mountain, most of the water it held is gone. This dried air moves down the mountainsides, bringing little or no rain to the lowlands, which become deserts.

Extra, Extra Dry   Not only is the air coming over the mountainside dry, but it can actually dry out the land! The air heats up as it reaches the warm earth. This increases its capacity to hold water. So it soaks up water from the land.

Interior Dryness   In the heart of northern Africa, you'll find the largest desert in the world: the Sahara. This desert lies in the continent's interior, far from areas where the ocean winds carry rain. Like other interior deserts in Australia and Mongolia, the Sahara rarely receives the ocean's moisture. By the time the winds arrive here, they've already dropped their rain elsewhere.

Cold Currents   On the west coasts of South America and Southern Africa, and on Mexico's Baja California peninsula, dry deserts extend to the oceanside. Here ocean winds are cooled as they blow across very cold currents near shore. As this cooled air can hold very little water, it doesn't pick up much moisture from the ocean. Dry and cool, this air blows inland, creating a desert. Occasionally currents shift and carry fog inland, which is why these deserts are sometimes called fog deserts. But even though there's fog, very little of this moisture falls as rain. Creatures who live in these deserts find unique ways of collecting water from the fog. A beetle species in the Namib Desert angles its back into incoming fog so that water droplets gather on its back then run down into its mouth.

A COMBINATION OF FACTORS

In some cases, more than one process helps form a desert. The deserts in North America are in the rain shadow of the Sierra Nevada Range. But the southern portions are also in the subtropics. Both factors dry these areas. Still other desert areas are being created and expanded not because of the processes above, but because of people's activities (*see* chapter 7).

DESERT SOILS

Desert soils vary. They can be white, black, red, brown, sandy, crumbly, chalky, or full of clay. In general, desert soils are mineral-rich. But they have less organic matter— decayed plants and animals—than most soils. This is because there are fewer plants and animals in deserts to start with.

Desert Pavement   Some deserts don't have much soil at all. They may have a solid rock surface. Or, if wind has blown small particles away, a desert can develop a pebbly rock surface, called "desert pavement." Looking like a strange cobbled street, this desert pavement stretches for hundreds of miles in the Sahara and Gobi deserts.

Salt   Some deserts have salty lakes or salty soils. Some of this salt comes from underground when rainwater dissolves salt deep in the soil, then moves it up to the surface during evaporation. Salt can also come from surrounding mountains. Water flows through the mountains, picks up

A salt crust remains in Death Valley National Monument, California, where the waters of a shallow lake evaporated 2,000 years ago.

salts, and flows into valleys, forming lakes. As water evaporates, the salt becomes concentrated. In some cases the lakes dry up completely, leaving a salt crust that ranges from a few inches to a few miles thick.

Desert Varnish, Desert Cement, and Living Soil   Desert soils have some unusual features. Windblown and rain-dissolved particles can create a dark sheen—called desert varnish—on the surface of rocks. Some minerals cement desert soil together. This forms "hardpans"—a hard crust that makes the soil less permeable to rainwater. And in parts of the desert, tiny plants such as algae and small, plantlike organisms such as lichen create a fragile, living crust on the soil.

LANDS OF CHANGE

For thousands of years, people have reported hearing loud cracking noises in the desert. Recent travelers compare the noises to gunshots. It turns out that this sound is none other than natural weathering at work. With the rapid heating and cooling of the desert, rocks expand and contract, building up strain. This strain can build up until a rock cracks—loudly and without warning.

Water and Wind   Even though the desert is usually dry, water is one of its most important weathering agents, particularly in semi-arid deserts. Storms cause floods that carry rocks ranging from sand-size to boulder-size. Flood waters running down mountains drop their load of sediment, forming alluvial fans. Wind also plays a role, moving sand bit by bit, forming dunes that look like frozen waves. The result is a startling array of landforms unique to the desert biome.

Dunes (left) are formed by wind sculpting desert sand.
Buttes (right) are created by a combination of wind and rain.   **23**

SKY ISLANDS

Right in the middle of some deserts, you can find patches of other biomes. These "islands" of forest and grassland are up on mountains. They exist because temperature and other conditions vary with altitude. Just by climbing these mountains, you can go from desert at the bottom, to grassland, then to evergreen woodland, and pine and fir forest at the very top.

BUILD YOUR OWN HYGROMETER

How humid is the air where you live? Here's how you can build your own hygrometer and find out. A hygrometer measures relative humidity—the ratio of the amount of water in the air to the amount the air can actually hold at that temperature.

First, you'll need:
- 2 thermometers
- 2 rubber bands
- Some cotton
- A shallow pan of water
- 2 pieces of string
- An eyedropper or spoon

1. Divide the cotton into two equal pieces. Using a rubber band, attach each piece of cotton to the bottom end of each thermometer. Twirl the cotton on the end of each to make a wick.

2. Indoors or outdoors, hang the thermometers in the shade so that:
- They are suspended at the same height;
- The tip of the cotton on thermometer #2 is in the water in the pan.

Neither of the thermometers is actually in the water. The cotton will wick water up to keep thermometer #2 wet.

CHART A: RELATIVE HUMIDITY TABLE FOR FAHRENHEIT READINGS

Temperature Difference (in °F)	Dry-Bulb Temperature					
	100°–90°	89°–80°	79°–70°	69°–60°	59°–50°	49°–40°
1	96	96	95	95	94	93
2	92	92	91	90	88	86
3	89	88	86	85	82	78
4	86	84	82	80	76	71
5	82	80	78	75	70	64
6	79	76	74	70	65	57
7	76	73	70	65	59	50
8	72	70	66	61	54	44
9	69	66	62	56	49	38
10	66	62	58	52	43	31
15	52	46	40	31	19	
20	38	32	24	12		
25	27	26	9			
30	16	8				

3. Use an eyedropper or spoon to soak the entire lump of cotton on thermometer #2 with water. This will begin the wicking action.

4. Wait one hour. Read and record the thermometer temperatures.

To find the relative humidity using your readings: if you are using a Fahrenheit thermometer, use Chart A; if you are using a Celsius thermometer, use Chart B. Choose the column that corresponds to your dry-bulb temperature. Then subtract your wet-bulb temperature reading from your dry-bulb temperature reading. Read down the left side of the chart to find your temperature difference and move across to

CHART B: RELATIVE HUMIDITY TABLE FOR CELSIUS READINGS

Temperature Difference (in °C)	Dry-Bulb Temperature				
	37°–33°	32°–28°	27°–23°	22°–18°	17°–15°
1	93	93	92	91	90
2	87	86	84	83	81
3	81	79	77	74	71
4	75	73	70	66	63
5	69	67	63	59	54
6	64	61	57	51	46
7	59	55	50	44	38
8	54	50	44	37	30
9	49	44	39	31	23
10	44	39	33	24	15
11	40	35	28	18	8
12	36	30	22	12	
13	32	25	17	6	
14	28	21	12		
15	24	17	8		

the column that corresponds to your dry-bulb temperature. That number represents relative humidity.

5. Check the thermometers each hour for several hours. Be sure there's enough water in the pan to keep the wick of thermometer #2 wet.

Hygrometers measure relative humidity because water evaporates quicker from a wet-bulb thermometer when the air is dry. In a wet environment, evaporation takes longer because the air is already "full" of water vapor. The faster water evaporates from the wet thermometer bulb, the more heat will be removed from the thermometer, cooling it off and giving a lower temperature.

✤ 4 ✤
DESERT PLANTS

With dry air, little rainfall, and searing heat, a desert hardly seems like a good spot for plants to grow. In many ways it's not. Deserts may go for years without rain, then get several inches in a day. What rain does arrive can rush over the desert soil, with only a little water soaking into the ground where a plant's roots can absorb it.

An unprotected plant can easily dry out, or desiccate, in dry desert air. Hot sun can raise a plant's internal temperature too high for photosynthesis to occur—even to the point where the plant's tissues literally cook. Cold, too, can be a danger. Winter temperatures in a cold desert can dip to -40°F (-40°C). A plant's inner fluids can freeze, expanding to form ice that ruptures the plant's cell walls.

Deserts, however, do have their advantages. They receive lots of sunshine—a natural energy source that plants use to make their own food. Some desert soils are rich with the minerals necessary for plant growth. But they are likely to be short on organic matter. Plants need this organic matter because it provides nitrogen and helps the soil hold water.

All in all, the desert is a challenging place for plant survival. Yet for thousands of years plant species have adapted and thrived in these arid lands.

WATER GATHERING AND STORAGE

One way plants handle dry spells is to gather lots of water when it's plentiful, then store it.

Reaching Roots   Desert plants may seem small, few, and far between. But there's often more to these plants than meets the eye. Below ground, desert plants may have 2 to 10 times as much tissue as they do aboveground. Fanning out below the soil's surface, or reaching down deep, these roots help gather as much rainwater as possible.

Some desert plants have long roots called "taproots." One or more of these roots grows deep into the soil and gathers water from underground streams. A mesquite tree's taproot can reach down as much as 100 feet (30 meters). This gives the mesquite tree access to a water supply that's more reliable than surface rainfall.

Swell Stems   Ever notice that some desert plants look fat? Cacti and other desert plants store large amounts of water in their roots, leaves, and stems. These kinds of plants are called succulents. Scientists estimate that a mature saguaro cactus can hold six tons of water in its trunk! Its pleated design allows the cactus to swell with water during rainy periods. Then, during dry periods, it shrinks as water is used up.

Life Along a Wash   Along the banks of dried desert streams, or washes, you may see cottonwoods, willows, and other trees. These plants could not survive in other, drier parts of the desert. But the large volumes of water they receive during floods, and water underneath the ground, can keep them alive year-round. Sand dunes are also among the wettest desert sites, because water percolates down into the dune sand more easily than it does in many desert soils.

• SAGUARO CACTI: THE SLOW-GROWING GIANTS •

The saguaro starts as a seed smaller than a grain of sand. Yet it can grow to be 50 feet (15 meters) high and weigh over 8 tons (7 metric tons). This transformation doesn't happen overnight, of course. It's a year or two before the cactus is a quarter of an inch (0.6 centimeter) high. Fifteen more years pass before it's a foot (30 centimeters) tall. It's 65 to 75 years old before it can form branches. These desert old-timers can get to be 150 to 200 years old.

In cartoons, saguaros have two branches pointing up, like outlaws with their hands raised. But real saguaros can have up to 50 arms that curl and point in various directions. Supporting this much plant growth is no easy feat. Shallow roots spreading out from the saguaro's base can absorb 200 gallons (760 liters) of water from a single rain. This water is stored in its pleated trunk, which can swell to hold water then shrink as it is used up.

A saguaro produces about 40 million seeds in its lifetime. Yet scientists estimate only one of those seeds will become a full-sized, adult saguaro. Most seeds are eaten by animals.

Young saguaros grow best if they sprout under a "nurse" tree. This tree shades the young saguaro from damaging sun, drying winds, and animals that might trample it.

Over the past century, in some areas, the largest mature saguaros have been dying off faster than young ones have replaced them. This may be because of unusually cold weather; frost can kill this species, which live farther north than other columnar cacti. Other factors are also involved. Overgrazing can eliminate nurse trees the saguaros need, lightning kills some trees, and cactus "rustlers" illegally collect and sell cacti for landscaping.

The saguaro cactus, which bears the state flower
of Arizona, is protected by law.

REDUCING WATER LOSS

Getting water is only half the battle—the other half is keeping it.

Smaller Surfaces   One noticeable difference between cacti and other plants is their lack of leaves—at least what you and I might recognize as leaves. Broad, thin leaves are good surfaces for collecting light and air for photosynthesis. But a leaf surface is also a place to lose water. And water is precious in the desert.

That's why cacti carry out photosynthesis not in leaves, but in their thick stems. Thick stems are less likely to dry out. These stems have less surface area than broad, thin leaves. That means there's less area where wind, heat, and dry air can contact their tissues and evaporate water. A cactus's spines are actually modified leaves.

Sealing Wax   Plants can lose water directly through their surfaces. To combat this water loss, desert plants such as the creosote bush have a waxy coating that seals in water.

Closable and Disposable Leaves   During the hottest part of the day, mesquite trees fold their leaves. Why? To reduce water loss. The ocotillo does the job another way. It sprouts its leaves only after rain. As the soil dries, and water is depleted, the leaves wither and fall. The ocotillo remains leafless until the next rain.

The Night Club   In order to produce food by photosynthesis, plants need to take in carbon dioxide and give off oxygen. They do this through stomates—pores in the plant's surface. But on a hot, windy desert day, a plant with

Like many desert plants, when the ocotillo blooms depends on when rain arrives.

open pores could be in danger. Its fluids could easily evaporate through these tiny openings.

To combat this problem, some desert plants open their stomates only at night. At night the desert is cooler and evaporation is less rapid. During the cool dark hours these plants produce and store carbon dioxide they will use during the day. The rest of the photosynthetic process occurs during daylight hours, when the sun's energy is available to drive the chemical reactions.

PERFECT TIMING

At certain times of the year you can see hundreds of daisies, lilies, snapdragons, and other flowering annuals in the desert. These fragile-looking flowers might seem out of place in harsh desert conditions. In fact, these plants aren't adapted to live in very dry soils. To avoid dry conditions, these plants come and go very quickly. After a heavy rain, they sprout, quickly grow, flower, and produce seed. All this happens in 6 to 8 weeks; the rest of the year these plants' seeds lie dormant in the desert soil.

Some seeds will not germinate after just a light rain. Their seed coat contains a chemical growth inhibitor that must be washed off for the seed to germinate. Other seeds have a seed coat that must be physically worn away—as it would be when tumbled along in a desert flood—in order to germinate.

PROTECTION AND DEFENSE

In the desert, as in other biomes, plants have adapted to protect themselves from plant eaters, harsh weather, and other plants that might push into their living space.

Special Spines Spines protect cacti from not only grazing animals, but also from the sun, wind, and in some cases, cold. Some cacti have silvery spines that reflect light, protecting their tissues from the sun. Spines also break the wind, reducing evaporation. In a few species, mats of spines trap air against the cactus. This blanket of air protects the plant from cold nighttime temperatures.

The jumping cholla's spines help it "hitchhike" to new areas. When an animal brushes against it, spiny sections of cactus break off. These pieces can remain attached to the animal as it travels to other areas. Then the cactus pieces may fall off or be scraped off the animal and take root and grow.

Chemical Warfare If you've ever visited a desert, you may notice that the plants are fewer and farther apart than in some other biomes. This is probably caused in part by scarce resources. But plants also take an active role in keeping their "space." Scientists suspect that many desert plants secrete chemicals into the soil to inhibit the growth of other plants nearby.

CLINGING TO LIFE

No doubt about it. Plants have some amazing adaptations for desert conditions. Even deep in desert soils, and inside rocks, there are plants: tiny green algae. No one's quite sure how they got there, or how they survive. Yet somehow they cling to life.

Still, it's important to remember that the North American desert contains much more plant life than most other deserts around the world. Plants do not grow in every desert. Vast stretches of rocky, pebbly, and sandy desert have little or no vegetation. It's for good reason that deserts are considered some of the harshest lands on earth.

⚜ 5 ⚜
DESERT ANIMALS

Gulping fog, seeking shade, or swimming through the sand, desert animals have some impressive ways of handling the challenges of desert life. Like plants, they need to beat the heat, get water, stay warm on cool nights, and unburnt on sunny days. But unlike plants, they can't send down a taproot for water or a web of roots to catch rain. And they can't make their own food using photosynthesis.

Still, animals do have one big advantage: they can move around. Lizards waddle into the sun to warm up, then shift to the shade to cool down. Bats migrate hundreds of miles so they can sip the nectar of many different plants in bloom. And vultures fly high, where the air temperature is cooler and they can get a better view of the ground.

But moving around isn't the only way animals cope with desert conditions. Spadefoot toads lay low, spending nine or more months underground. Fairy shrimp and brine shrimp deposit eggs that can survive 25 years in a dried-out lake bed, then hatch and wriggle to life when water arrives. And these are just two out of the thousands of remarkable adaptations desert creatures exhibit.

WATER STRATEGIES
In the desert, animals get water when and where they can. African and Asian sandgrouse fly to desert oases, where they drink their fill and soak their feathers. Then they travel

Powerful hind legs allow the kangaroo rat to make the kangaroolike leaps that give it its name.

as far as 40 miles (60 kilometers) back to their nests, where their thirsty chicks sip water from the parents' feathers.

Food and Drink   For many desert animals, a meal is both food and drink. Seeds can be 20 to 50 percent water, enough to help quench the thirst of plant eaters. And an animal's body may be as much as 75 percent water, so meat eaters can get water from their food, too.

Water Makers   Animals such as the kangaroo rat actually make water in their bodies, as a by-product of the food they eat. As a result, a kangaroo rat may go its whole life without a sip of water. Other animals, such as the desert cockroach, can extract water directly from the air, even at humidities as low as 50 percent.

Lumps and Humps   No, a camel's hump isn't filled with water as many people believe. It is made of fat. As this fat is

· SPADEFOOT TOAD ·

Amphibians have moist skin and need water to reproduce. So you'd hardly expect to find them in a desert. But a few specially adapted toads do live in the deserts of the American southwest. Couch's spadefoot toad spends nine months of the year underground. It lives in a burrow dug with its spade-shaped back feet. A special skin casing helps it retain some of its body moisture.

When the rainy season arrives, the vibrations of raindrops hitting the dirt awaken these toads. They dig their way out, eat their fill of insects, find a mate, lay eggs, and soon afterward, dig back down underground. It's a race against time for the eggs to hatch and develop before the rainy season puddles dry up. Not all of the tadpoles make it in time.

converted into body fuel, it releases water. A typical 90-pound (41-kilogram) hump can be converted to 12 gallons (45 liters) of water. This fat helps the camel get through thirsty times. But perhaps even more important, the hump is part of a complex body system that helps prevent camels from overheating and thereby using up too much water to cool themselves off.

Water Conservation   In the desert, even those animals that can get water need to keep all they can. Many desert animals have superefficient kidneys and other adaptations that minimize the amount of water they lose in their urine. Camels supercool their nostrils so water will condense in them and can be reabsorbed from the air being exhaled.

Just Add Water . . .   Nematodes, a type of worm, enter a resting state in which they can dry up, but do not die. Just add water, and they become active again. It's a handy adaptation for the desert. Brine shrimp, fairy shrimp, and some African fish lay eggs that can survive even 25 years of drought.

BODY HEAT

As far as body heat goes, animals naturally fall into two categories: endothermic, or warm-blooded, and ectothermic, or cold-blooded. Endothermic animals, such as birds and mammals, are internally heated. They use the energy from the food they eat to maintain a constant body temperature. Ectothermic creatures, such as reptiles, amphibians, and insects, rely on the environment to help them control their temperature. A lizard, for instance, can warm its body with the warmth from hot air, sunlight, or a warm rock.

Ectothermic creatures have some advantages in the desert. They can survive with a wider range of body temperatures than birds and mammals. And since they don't use energy on "central heating," they don't need to eat as much food. At 100°F (38°C), a rodent would have to use seven times as much energy to keep its body going as a lizard would for the same amount of body weight. Mammals generally breathe more, lose more water, and have to eat more to run their body processes.

With this much of an advantage, you might think the desert would be full of nothing but snakes, lizards, scorpions, and insects. Fact is, there are lots of these creatures in the desert. But some mammals and birds have adapted, too. They have developed ways to beat the heat and reduce the stress on their bodies.

BEATING THE HEAT

One good way to beat the desert heat is to avoid it. Rattlesnakes, kit foxes, and kangaroo rats spend most of the day resting in underground burrows. While the soil surface up top may be 165°F (74°C), their underground dens may

HOW TEMPERATURE VARIES WITH DEPTH UNDERGROUND		
	Cold Winter Day	Hot Summer Day
Surface	20°F (-8°C)	165°F (74°C)
1 foot down (30.5 cm)	40°F (4.4°C)	105°F (41°C)
2 feet down (60.9 cm)	50°F (10°C)	95°F (35°C)
3 feet down (91.4 cm)	60°F (16°C)	85°F (29°C)
4 feet down (121.9 cm)	62°F (17°C)	83°F (28°C)

Courtesy of the Arizona-Sonora Desert Museum

be a livable 80°F (27°C). Resting quietly, these animals can conserve their energy for nighttime hunting or seed-gathering expeditions.

Hot Footing It   The ground's surface is often 30°F to 40°F (18°C to 24°C) hotter than the air temperature. No wonder some desert lizards are always "hot footing" it. They run on their hind legs to keep their bodies and front feet off the hot sand. In the heat of the day, lizards climb up in shrubs because it's cooler even a few inches off the ground.

Natural Radiators   The big ears of desert hares, rabbits, and foxes help them focus sounds and hear better. But big ears also help them cool off. Ears, long legs, and bare patches of skin where blood vessels are close to the surface act as natural radiators. Blood circulating through these spots radiates heat to the surrounding air. This cools the animal off.

Wet fur or skin can cool an animal even more. That's why kangaroo rats lick their fur, foxes pant, and birds move their throats to evaporate water from their lungs and mouths. All these animals make use of evaporative cooling.

The water on their skin absorbs their body heat. As it evaporates, it takes some of that heat away from their bodies and into the air.

OTHER ADAPTATIONS

Of course there's more to an animal's life than just finding water and escaping the heat. There's also searching for food, evading predators, and reproducing. Here are a few ways desert animals accomplish these tasks:

Animal Hoarders   To guard themselves against unpredictable desert food supplies, some animals stock up. Harvester ants and kangaroo rats store bushels of seeds in underground burrows for times of scarcity. Loggerhead shrikes catch lizards and then leave them hanging on cactus spines, ready for later consumption. Some honeypot ants become living storage bottles. They're stuffed full of sweet liquid. Then they crawl into the ant colony's burrow and hang upside down, storing the liquid food for hard times.

Waiting for a Meal   When there isn't enough food around, some animals just go to sleep. Pocket mice, kangaroo rats, and some ground squirrels and birds enter a state called torpor and may remain in that state for months. In torpor their breathing and other body processes slow down, saving energy. By saving energy, they need less food. This helps them survive until the time when food is plentiful once again.

Sidewinders   Ever tried running fast across dry, loose sand? The sand shifts, giving you very little traction. Sand-dune inhabitants have the same problem. So, snakes called sidewinders lick this problem by moving sideways in an S shape, anchoring their bodies on one coil and throwing the other. This motion has an added benefit: the snake's body touches the hot sand in fewer places, so it's less likely to get burned.

Very Venomous   Next time you're in the desert, wear good boots and watch where you put your hands and feet. You don't want to surprise any venomous snakes, lizards, spiders, or scorpions that may be resting in shady nooks and crannies under rocks and logs. Venom helps desert predators subdue their prey quickly, with a minimum amount of energy. Fortunately, what is deadly to a small prey animal is usually fairly harmless to an animal the size of a human. However, several scorpion and snake species in the southwestern United States can deliver painful, poisonous bites. These bites are dangerous and occasionally deadly to people, especially small children.

A sidewinder leaves distinctive tracks in the sand.

6

DESERT COMMUNITIES

Desert animals and plants don't adapt just to heat, cold, and dryness. Over thousands of years, they have adapted to one another, forming tightly woven communities. Scientists who study these communities and their relationship to the physical environment are called ecologists.

GOING WITH THE FLOW

Energy flow is one of the things that ties the animals and plants in a desert community to one another. Energy in the form of sunlight is used by plants to make sugars, which in turn are stored as starch. These sugars become part of the plant's leaves, roots, and shoots. Then, when these plant parts are eaten, they become part of what eats them. At each step, some of the energy is passed on, and some is dissipated as heat. In the next step some of the energy becomes part of an animal who eats the animal that ate the plants. When that animal dies, the scavenger that eats its dead body gains energy. And so on. Finally, decomposers, microbes that break down dead plants and animals into soil, acquire part of the energy in the dead plants and animals.

Food Webs   One way ecologists show a community's energy flow is through food chains and food webs. A food chain shows what one type of animal eats and what its prey eats in turn. A food web goes a step further, showing the relationships among many animals in a community. It

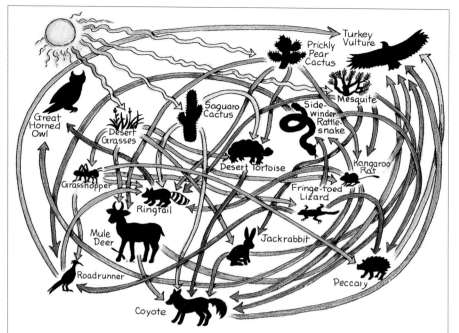

A food web shows the transfer of energy from the sun to plants, then to plant eaters (herbivores), and finally to meat eaters (carnivores).

shows who eats what and who eats whom within a community. Although the food-web diagram here may look complex, it is actually greatly simplified. A web that included all the animals and plants in a small patch of the Chihuahuan Desert would have hundreds of strands!

Food Pyramids   Even a food web doesn't tell the whole story. After all, it takes more than one desert cottontail to satisfy a coyote's appetite day after day. And each cottontail eats more than one plant. Ecologists express these energy quantities in an energy pyramid. The pyramid shows how many producers—plants—are needed to feed the primary consumers—mice—that are needed to feed the secondary consumers—snakes—that are needed to feed the top predator—a coyote. Looking at the pyramid, you can see why there needs to be more mice than coyotes in the desert.

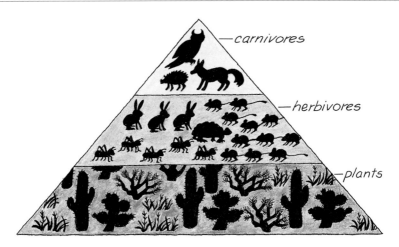

An energy pyramid shows how many plants (primary producers) are needed to feed the herbivores (primary consumers), which in turn are needed to feed the carnivores (secondary consumers).

Still, no desert community—no natural community, in fact—is quite this simple. A coyote may eat fruit one day and eat a kangaroo rat or a desert cottontail the next. A kangaroo rat may become the meal of a snake, which becomes the meal of a roadrunner, which is then a meal for a coyote. It's no wonder ecologists have a tough job figuring out how the desert works. It's a never-ending challenge.

THE MEASURES OF LIFE

If you took all the plants in a square mile or square kilometer of desert and piled them up on a scale, how much would they all weigh? It's hard to say. Yet this is the kind of thing ecologists try to measure, at least for small areas. The weight of plant matter—roots, shoots, and so on, for a certain area—is called plant biomass. Ecologists use biomass figures to compare the productivity of deserts with that of other biomes. In general, deserts are much less productive than most other biomes. A desert's plant biomass is 270 to 2,700 pounds per acre (300 to 3,000 kilograms per hectare) while a temperate forest's biomass can be 80,000 pounds per acre (89,600 kilograms per hectare)!

Diversity Another important measure of a biome is species diversity. Species diversity is how many different kinds of animals and plants live in a place. Rain forests have lots of different kinds of plants and animals—an extremely high species diversity. Very dry deserts, such as the Sahara, have noticeably low species diversity. But semi-arid areas in the Sonora, Mojave, and Chihuahuan deserts generally have fairly high species diversity.

CLOSE RELATIONSHIPS

Over the years, desert animals and plants have developed some surprising relationships. In some of these relationships, both parties benefit. For instance, the organ-pipe cactus flowers at night so bats can pollinate it. The bats, in return, get the cactus's nourishing nectar. This kind of relationship is called mutualism.

Another kind of relationship, called commensalism, gives one party the benefit, without really harming the other. A good example is elf owls, who take over the abandoned nest cavities of woodpeckers. Yet another type of relationship is parasitism, a relationship where one party benefits and the other is harmed. An example is the botfly that plagues desert bighorn sheep. Botfly larvae live within the sheep's horns, eating its tissues. Dead larvae in the horns become a breeding ground for bacteria that eat away the sheep's skull and cause brain damage. Desert bighorn sheep began having these botflies when people started grazing domestic sheep, that had the parasite, nearby. This parasite is now devastating many bighorn populations.

SIMILAR SOLUTIONS

Like crazy pinballs, jerboas in Africa and kangaroo rats in North America zigzag across the desert. Both species are

• WHAT A RAT'S NEST! •

Have you ever been called a "packrat" because you collected too much stuff? Well, the collecting habits of *real* packrats are proving useful to scientists. Packrats collect seeds, stems, rocks, bones—almost anything—and place them in their underground dens. Over the years, the nests' contents become cemented together. Generation after generation, packrats occupy the same nest sites. Their nests can pile up for thousands of years!

Scientists study the contents of these ancient nests to find clues about how an area looked thousands of years ago. By studying rat nests, scientists have discovered that pinyon and juniper trees once grew in what are today the Sonora and Chihuahuan deserts. Mammoths, camels, and sloths lived there, too. Scientists now believe these deserts are very young. They have existed for only 10,000 years or less.

---

small and furry and hop on their hind legs. Yet they aren't closely related. Neither are the Saharan horned vipers and the Sonoran sidewinders, though these snakes travel with the same sidewinding motion. All these animals are examples of convergent evolution. They live in deserts in different parts of the world. But they separately evolved similar forms. In each case these animals developed the same solutions to the challenges of desert life.

DESERTS THROUGH THE AGES

Cave paintings in the Sahara show that elephants, giraffes, and other animals once lived there. Yet these animals don't live in deserts. How is this possible? Well, what is now the Sahara wasn't always desert. Over thousands and millions of years, changes in climate shifted the locations of deserts. Also, continents gradually moved, causing deserts to form and disappear, depending on the conditions at their new

45

locations. As these conditions changed, so did the communities of animals and plants that lived in them.

TAKE A HIKE IN THE DESERT

If you take a hike in the desert during the day, don't forget to wear sturdy boots, a hat with a brim, and suntan lotion on any bare skin. Lightweight long pants and a longsleeve shirt can help prevent sunburn and dehydration. Know where you're going, tell someone of your plans, and bring a map. And carry at least a gallon (about four liters) of water per person. If you get overheated, rest in the shade. Don't ration your water. The best place to store water is in your stomach. Sometimes by the time you feel really thirsty, you may already be on your way to dehydration.

To see the most wildlife, it's best to hike in the evening or early morning. Here are just a few of the things you can look for, smell for, and listen for on a Sonora Desert hike:

- Cuplike nests tucked in cholla cacti, where cactus wrens raise their young;
- Mounds where kangaroo rats live;
- Lizards basking on rocks;
- Young saguaro cacti growing under "nurse" trees, such as paloverdes;
- Shallow pits in the ground where peccaries have been digging for roots;
- Cavities in cacti, where woodpeckers or owls nest;
- A skunky odor, which may mean there are peccaries around;
- A dry rattle, which means you've gotten too close to a rattlesnake;
- A broken-off piece of jumping cholla cactus, which may stick to your socks;
- A gorgeous pink and purple sunset—deserts have some of the best!

✳ 7 ✳
PEOPLE AND THE DESERT

If you're thirsty, just dig up a frog. A special Australian frog. Then squeeze the water from the frog and its water-filled "casing" right into your mouth. At least that's one way Australian Aborigines got their water in tough times. Personally, I'd recommend you bring enough water with you. Leave the frogs alone.

Still, knowing where to get water in drought times—from a toad, a tuber, or the trunk of a tree—is important. It's the kind of knowledge that has helped people survive in the desert for thousands of years.

ANCIENT DESERT PEOPLE

Some desert people stay alive by staying on the move—they are called nomads. Australian Aborigines follow the rains. They hunt animals and gather the plants that are plentiful during each season of the year. In the Sahara, Tuaregs live in tents and herd livestock such as sheep and goats. By shifting their herds to new grazing areas, they avoid overgrazing the land.

Farmers The Hopi and the Tohono O'odham of North America are desert farmers. Over thousands of years they have developed ways of farming in dry soils. They plant their crops along desert washes, where water remains underground even after rivers have dried up. And they

• NATIVE AMERICAN USES OF DESERT PLANTS •

• Barrel cactus grows slightly curved, and pointing south. This occurs because the cactus grows faster on its northern, shadier side than on its southern, sunnier side. People who know this can use the cactus, like a compass, to point them in the right direction.

• The Chihuahuan Desert's leather-plant, also called *sangre de drago*—blood of the dragon—contains a reddish juice traditionally used to treat eye and gum diseases.

• Aloe and jojoba, used in shampoos, burn remedies, and cosmetics, are the juices of desert plants.

• Creosote bush smells so pungent after rain that desert residents call it *hediondilla*, or "little stinker." This plant's resins protect it from ultraviolet light and from grazing animals that dislike the resins' taste. Creosote is used in Native American herbal medicines.

• The Tohono O'odham people of southwest Arizona make wine and jelly from the saguaro's reddish, sugary fruit.

• The fruit of the prickly pear cactus can be made into jam. Its young, flattened stems, called pads, can be boiled and eaten as vegetables.

• Ocotillo branches are used as fenceposts and to construct walls. When stuck into the ground, these branches can sprout and grow, forming living fences and walls.

• Saguaro spines were once used as sewing needles.

supplement their diets with animals, roots, leaves, and fruits gathered from the wild.

Today, many desert natives no longer practice their traditional ways of life. They don't rely on desert farming or a nomadic lifestyle. Fortunately, however, some still carry on their traditions. They're even teaching anthropologists and ecologists secrets of desert living that may help improve modern farming and medicine.

A member of the Hopi tribe plants corn in the traditional way.

PEOPLE IN THE DESERT TODAY

With sunny days, warm temperatures, and spectacular sunsets, America's desert southwest is a popular place to live, especially for retired persons. In the last decade population growth in the desert southwest has been one of the highest in the United States. This increase in population is overtaxing the desert's scarce water supply. More and more desert is being paved over and developed for homes, shopping malls, and businesses. Acres of desert are cleared and irrigated for golf courses.

Water Users In Las Vegas, Nevada, gigantic fountains spout water high into the air. You'd hardly know the city is in the middle of a desert. This and other desert cities and farms use river water and groundwater for their needs. This water has helped desert cities to grow. But consider these facts:

- So much water is pumped out of the Colorado River that some years, when the Colorado River reaches Mexico, it's barely a trickle! It used to be much more. What water does arrive is very salty and polluted with pesticides.

- People are now drinking water that took hundreds and thousands of years to build up underground. Yet this water is being used up in a matter of decades. Overuse of groundwater lowers the water level, putting it out of reach of desert plants' taproots.

Water Watchers Cities such as Tucson, Arizona, are starting to face up to their water troubles. New laws require water-saving devices: low-flow faucets and showerheads, for example. They also xeriscape—landscape with desert plants that require less water than grass lawns and exotic trees. And some cities have "water patrols," who search the city for people who are using too much water and either warn or fine them. All these actions are a good start. But water rights—who can use how much water and from where—promises to remain a controversial issue in the coming years.

ARE YOU A WATER WASTER?

Each year people waste millions of gallons of fresh, drinkable water. Conserving fresh water isn't just important for people in desert areas; it's important for people in all biomes. While salty, ocean water is plentiful on our planet, unpolluted, drinkable, fresh water is relatively scarce. The more we draw from rivers and underground sources, the less unpolluted water is available for wildlife and plants.

Here are some things you can do to conserve water:

- **Take the toothbrushing test** Next time you brush your teeth, put a bowl or pitcher in the sink to catch all the water used while you're brushing. See how much water you waste. (Many people leave the water running while they're brushing.) If you use a lot of water, develop a new habit for yourself, such as turning off the faucet while brushing, or using a cup of water you pour at the very beginning. Do whatever works best for you and saves water, too!

- **Try the leaky-toilet test**   According to one study, one out of five home toilets leaks. Does yours? If so, it can waste an estimated 4.3 gallons (16.3 liters) of water each day per person who uses it. Some leaky toilets may waste over 50 gallons (190 liters) of water per day! Here's how to check for leaks: Lift the lid off the toilet tank, not the bowl. Put 8 to 10 drops of red or blue food coloring in the water, then wait 20 minutes. (Don't use or flush the toilet during this time!) If any of the color shows up in the toilet bowl, your toilet leaks. Get it fixed! Be sure after this experiment is finished to flush the toilet to get the food coloring out of the tank and bowl.

- **Check your faucets**   Even the drips from one faucet can really add up. If you have a drippy faucet, use a watch with a second hand to see how often drips occur. One drip per second can waste over 10 gallons (40 liters) per day. Using the timing of your drips and the previous statistic, can you estimate how much water your faucet wastes? Get drippy faucets fixed. Fixing faucets is sometimes only a matter of buying a new washer—an inexpensive rubber ring that you can replace in the faucet nozzle.

DESERT FARMING AND IRRIGATION

People have been irrigating land for hundreds of years. But never has it been done on such a large scale as today.

Billion-dollar Plumbing   Even rice—a crop that requires knee-deep water—is grown in America's deserts. This is made possible by dams, pumps, pipes, and channels that bring water to semi-arid land in California and Arizona. These water projects, funded by taxpayers, make water cheap and readily available to desert farmers.

Warm, sunny days and plenty of fertilizer make these farms and orchards extremely productive. Much of the produce eaten by people all over the United States comes from irrigated desert farms and orchards in California, Arizona, and Mexico. But this irrigation uses up scarce water resources in desert lands.

Salinization and the Toxic Build-up   As it flows over the land, irrigation water picks up chemicals, such as salt and selenium, that occur naturally in the soil. When water evaporates, the chemicals in it become concentrated. Eventually, soil can become so salty that regular crops won't grow in it. Selenium can build up to toxic levels. Farm runoff—filled with salt, selenium, and pesticides—can be harmful to wildlife. And farmers may have to abandon farms with salty or selenium-filled soils.

DESERTS IN DANGER
Certainly overdevelopment, overuse of water, and soil salinization are among the main threats to desert ecosystems. But several other activities may destroy natural desert areas as well.

Grazing   Too many grazing animals in too small an area or for too long a time can spell trouble. Grazers can eat so much that the plants can't grow back and eventually die. Without plant roots to hold it in place, soil blows or washes away. This erosion turns a productive grassland or desert into dry, lifeless land.

Mining   Deserts are full of mineral resources –gold, copper, uranium, silver, phosphate, and other minable minerals. These minerals are utilized for making products people

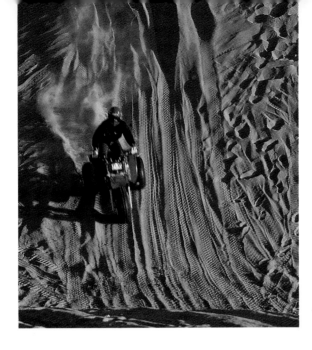

*Off-road vehicles
leave tracks
that can last
for decades in
the desert.*

use every day. But mining these minerals destroys parts of the desert.

Off-Road Vehicles   Jeeps, motorcycles, and other off-road vehicles (ORVs) can crush desert vegetation and scare wildlife or collapse their burrows. Many desert plants grow slowly and can't recover from such damage. Vehicle tracks can last for decades in dry desert conditions.

Collection of Plants and Animals   In some cases, desert animals and plants are being "loved" to death. Saguaro and other cacti are illegally removed from public lands and sold for thousands of dollars to enthusiastic collectors. Snakes are collected and used to make snakeskin boots, while many lizard species are sold as exotic pets.

DESERTIFICATION

In 100 countries around the world, deserts are spreading. Fifteen million acres (6 million hectares) of land become lifeless desert each year. This process, by which lands become dry, lifeless desert, is called desertification. Many people are worried about desertification. Why? Because it's not the "lush," semi-arid deserts such as the Sonora that are expanding their range. It's arid and hyper-arid, almost lifeless deserts that are taking up more and more of our planet's surface. And desertification can have a terrible human toll.

Many Causes One cause of desertification is climate change. Throughout the history of the earth, deserts have expanded and contracted as the earth became hotter and colder. And they've shifted as the earth's surface changed. But people's activities also cause desertification. Deforestation, livestock overgrazing, ORV use, mining, and other desert threats cause erosion. This erosion can turn grassland or a wildlife-filled desert into lifeless desert.

Scientists disagree over which of these factors—people or climate—is the main cause of current desertification. But even if climate change is the underlying cause, people's activities are certainly accelerating the process in many parts of the world. These climate changes also may be connected to global warming. Global warming is the predicted change in the world's climate as a result of air pollution released by cars, factories, volcanoes, and other pollution sources.

The Famine Connection Droughts—long periods without rain—make desertification worse. During droughts, crops fail. Plants that livestock depend on die. As a result, with no crops and few healthy animals, people starve. The remaining livestock overgraze bushes, trees, and whatever grass is left. People cut down the remaining trees for fuel. Soil blows away. All this adds to desertification. Grasslands, forests, and semi-arid deserts turn into arid and hyper-arid, almost lifeless desert land. Then, when the rains return, there is little fertile soil in which to grow plants. It's difficult

*Preserving the desert will insure a safe home for
desert creatures such as these peccaries.*

for the land and its people to recover. During past droughts, the Sahara has expanded by 30 miles (48 kilometers) per year.

THE FUTURE OF THE DESERT

Deserts ecosystems are fragile. At best, they only support a small number of plants and animals. Even those populations tend to change in size, with natural month-to-month and year-to-year rainfall fluctuations. Yet millions of humans—more than ever before in the earth's history— now live in the desert year-round. Can this many people live in the desert without destroying the desert's ecological balance? It remains to be seen.

SEEDS OF HOPE

There *is* hope for the future of the world's deserts. All over the globe, people are working to slow desertification and protect natural desert areas. Here are just a few of the things they are doing:

- Studying global climate change in order to understand how and why droughts occur;
- Planting trees in Kenya, China, and other countries, so the tree roots will hold the soil and decrease erosion;
- Learning about Native American dry farming, in hopes of drawing on their traditions to improve farming today;
- Developing new food crops that can grow in salty desert soils;
- Cutting down on water use by taking shorter showers, and using low-flow faucets, showerheads, and toilets;
- Passing better laws to protect existing desert lands, plants, and wildlife;
- Restricting off-road vehicle access to desert lands and helping ORV users learn where and when they can use their vehicles;
- Setting aside and preserving large areas of desert, such as the Mojave Desert, which is being considered as a site for a new national park.

These widespread, creative efforts to preserve desert areas are indeed bringing good results. But desert-caretakers say they still need help. Whether you live in a desert or not, you can join in their efforts. With many people working hard to preserve this remarkable biome, the future for desert wildlife and desert people will indeed be bright.

RESOURCES AND WHAT
YOU CAN DO TO HELP

Here's what you can do to help ensure that deserts are conserved:

• Learn more by reading books and watching videos and television programs about the desert. Check your local library, bookstore, and video store for resources. Here are just a few of the books available for further reading:

Arid Lands by Jake Page and the Editors of Time-Life Books (Planet Earth Series) (Time-Life, 1984).
Deserts by James A. MacMahon (The Audubon Society Nature Guides Series) (Alfred A. Knopf, 1985).
The Great Southwest Nature Factbook : A Guide to the Region's Remarkable Animals, Plants and Natural Features by Susan J. Tweit, (Alaska Northwest Books, 1992).
The Living Earth Book of Deserts by Susan Arritt (Reader's Digest, 1993).
The Mysterious Lands by Ann Haymond Zwinger (Truman Talley / Plume, 1989).

• For more information on deserts, write to the following organizations:

Arizona-Sonora Desert Museum
2021 North Kinnery Rd.
Tucson, AZ 85743

Chihuahuan Desert Research Institute
P. O. Box 1334
Alpine, TX 79831

Tucson Audubon Society
300 E. University Blvd.
Suite 120
Tucson, AZ 85705

• Join an environmental organization that works to protect deserts. For membership information, contact any of the following organizations:

The Desert Protective Council, Inc.
P. O. Box 4294
Palm Springs, CA 92263

National Audubon Society
700 Broadway
New York, NY 10003

National Parks and Conservation Association
1776 Massachusetts Ave., NW
Washington, DC 20036

The Nature Conservancy
1815 Lynn Street
Arlington, VA 22209

Sierra Club
730 Polk Street
San Francisco, CA 94109

The Wilderness Society
900 17th St. NW
Washington, DC 20006-2596

• To order desert-related books, posters, and other materials, write these companies and ask for information on their desert products:

Collamore Educational Publishing
DC Heath & Co Distribution Center
2700 N. Richardt Ave.
Indianapolis, IN 46219
(They sell an interactive computer program on deserts for Apple II, IBM, and Tandy computers)

Southwest Parks and Monuments Association
221 N. Court Ave.
Tucson, AZ 85701
(They sell books and booklets)

• Visit a museum, national park, national monument, or botanical garden that has desert features. The following desert parks are located in the United States:

Arches National Park, Moab, UT
Bandelier National Monument, Los Alamos, NM
Big Bend National Park, Big Bend National Park, TX
Canyon de Chelly National Monument, Chinle, AZ
Canyonlands National Park, Moab, UT
Capitol Reef National Park, Torrey, UT
Carlsbad Caverns National Park, Carlsbad, NM
Chiricahua National Monument, Willcox, AZ
Death Valley National Monument, Death Valley, CA
Grand Canyon National Park, Grand Canyon, AZ
Guadalupe Mountains National Park, Salt Flat, TX, near Carlsbad, NM
Joshua Tree National Monument, Twenty-Nine Palms, CA
Organ Pipe Cactus National Monument, Lukeville, AZ
Petrified Forest National Park, Holbrook, AZ
Saguaro National Monument, Tucson, AZ
White Sands National Monument, Alamogordo, NM
Zion National Park, Springdale, UT

• Find out where your water comes from. Then work to reduce your own water use. For a catalog of low-flow faucets, showerheads, and other conservation products, contact:

Real Goods
966 Mazzoni Street
Ukiah, CA 95482-3471

Seventh Generation
Colchester, VT
05446-1672

• If you live in a desert area, encourage your family, local landowners, or government officials to xeriscape—to plant native desert plants that don't use much water. This not only saves water, it can also attract wildlife such as hummingbirds and butterflies. If you buy desert plants, try to be sure they come from a greenhouse or nursery and have not been illegally taken from the wild.

• Avoid buying snakes and lizards that may have been taken from wild desert areas. If you have any doubt about the source of a pet, don't buy it. Purchase pets that are captive-bred, such as rabbits, cats, dogs, budgies, and guppies, not exotic animals that are more likely to have been taken from the wild.

• Write letters to state and national government officials, telling them you feel desert conservation is important.

• Reduce, reuse, and recycle: the fewer goods you use—from stereos to aluminum cans—the fewer resources have to be used to make them. Some of these resources come from minerals mined in deserts.

GLOSSARY

alluvial fan   a fan-shaped deposit of gravel, sand, and silt that forms where a stream flows into a plain and slows down, dropping its load

annuals   plants that last only one year or season and must start growing from seeds the next year or season

aridity   dryness (Scientists classify deserts as semi-arid, arid, or hyper-arid, depending on how much rain they receive.)

biome   an area that has a certain kind of climate and a certain kind of community of plants and animals

community   a group of plants and animals that live together and interact with one another

consumers   animals that cannot make their own food, but must eat plants and / or other animals

convergent evolution   the process by which distantly related animals or plants evolve similar structures independently; this can occur when animals adapt in similar ways to similar living conditions, such as those in deserts

decomposers   organisms that feed on the dead bodies of other organisms, breaking them down into simpler substances

desertification   the process by which productive land that supports life is turned into lifeless desert

desiccation   the process of losing water, of drying out

ecologist   a scientist who studies living things and how they interact with one another and their environment

ecosystem   the pattern of relationships among a group of living things and their physical environment

ectothermic   having a body temperature that is dependent on the environment and is not kept constant by internal regulation (Also called cold-blooded.)

endothermic   having a body temperature that is internally regulated and kept at a fairly constant level, without regard to the temperature of the environment (Also called warm-blooded.)

ghost rain   rain that never reaches the ground because it evaporates on contact with a low-lying layer of hot air

global warming   the predicted change in the earth's climate caused by the build-up of pollutants in the earth's atmosphere; the end results may be rising sea levels, and shifting weather patterns, *not* an overall global warming as once thought

groundwater   water that is underground, such as that held in deep underground rivers, streams, and porous rock layers

hygrometer   an instrument that measures relative humidity

nomads   people who do not settle in one place for long, but instead travel from place to place

plant biomass   the weight of all the plant matter—roots, shoots, stems and other plant parts—for a given area

predator   an animal that catches and eats other animals

producers   organisms such as plants that make their own food

rain shadow desert   desert that receives little rain because a mountain or mountains block its rain supply

salinization   the process of becoming salty

species diversity   the number of different kinds of plants and animals in a given place

succulents   plants with thick, fleshy leaves that store a lot of water

torpor   an inactive, sluggish state

xeriscape   to landscape in a way that conserves water by planting plants that need little water

INDEX